LIVING "THE" LIFE WITH A QUADRIPLEGIC

BY
LINDA FEIGHT

DEDICATION

I am very proud of my family! And I want to dedicate this book to them.

Jeremy Reed, our son, who is our first born and has brought such a joy to his daddy and I over the years. And even today as you walk with the Lord, Jeremy you put Him first in leading your own family as God would direct you. Loving and honoring your wife Amy Dawn daily. Both of you are raising two beautiful children, our grandchildren, Trenten and Savanna to love Jesus also. Jeremy, you and Amy have also had your marriage challenged with physical obstacles and I am so proud of how you are walking each day with eyes on the goal that God has set before you. Daddy was, and I am so very proud of all you have accomplished and look forward to what you will achieve in the future as a husband, a father and as a child of God. What an example you and Amy have shown to the community as you are led by our Father in Heaven allowing your light to shine for all to see.

Elisha Mae, our daughter, you too have brought to daddy and I such a joy. Your smile and laughter has brightened our lives from the day you were born. I would often pray over you to never lose that wonderful smile. And God has honored my prayer. For our family and all who know you, your laughter makes all our cloudy days disappear. Letting the light of Jesus shine through you makes you beautiful inside and out. Now as a newlywed to your husband Ryan, you have a chance to make a new beginning to pass on the light of Jesus. And I see both you and Ryan setting before you a race to the finish, honoring God in all you do. Our mother/daughter relationship and bond is so treasured by me. I never want to take advantage or for granted what God has blessed us with. Thank you for your love and support even in this book.

Also, a portion of this dedication needs to go to Robin's mother and father, Leta and Reed Feight. Without the two of you, I would never have had a chance to be blessed with Robin in my life. Thank you!

To my mother, Dorothy Metzler who was my prayer warrior in my life, my example of walking in the love of Christ no matter the circumstance. To my dad, Robert Metzler, his example was to be strong and to show respect to mankind with integrity and honesty.

And to our extended families, brothers, sisters, sister-n-laws, and brother-n-laws; thank you for supporting us in our difficult years with your prayers and continual love. Also,our community, friends and neighbors for financial support and spiritual wisdom, words cannot express the times we treasured these.

A special thank you to Deborah King for proof-reading my manuscript

FORWARD BY BRIAN LAKE

This book is the story of a compelling and heartfelt journey of an unspeakable love that kept a family together and gave them the strength to never give up, despite the insurmountable odds they faced.

It is the journey of one man and one woman's extraordinary love for and commitment to one another and to their children that kept them moving forward, despite the restrictions of a wheelchair. As you read these words you will be challenged by Robin's life to live a life that reflects the very nature of Jesus Christ... being a servant to all those that we come into contact with, whether known or unknown and to love them with the love of God.

You will read that in one unexpected moment Robin and Linda's and their family's lives changed forever. And with that change came the wrestling with their hope, their fears and their faith. Yet you will read of their determination to live life to the fullest, to serve a faithful God and to fulfill all that

He called them to do amidst the circumstances they were facing. Even after the accident, Robin remained the head of his family, leading them in a positive direction as the Lord led him, never giving in to his restrictions or allowing them to stop him or prevent him from fulfilling his God-given desires. You will laugh along with Linda and others as she shares some of the humorous and not so humorous predicaments that Robin got himself into attempting to fulfill those desires.

Robin's walk with the Lord is a testament to us all. His fierce faith and strength never allowed him to give up and "I can't" was never in his vocabulary. He always seemed to find a way. You will read how that faith and determination spread not only to Linda and their children and kept the family moving forward, but to each one that Robin came in contact with.

Robin was a true servant of the King and a spreader of God's wild fire everywhere he went. He touched the very core of your soul with his kindness, his gentleness and his love and sincerity. One meeting with Robin and you knew you had been in the presence of someone special and unique. His sense of humor was seen in the common, everyday tasks of life. Linda shares some of these times with us. His determination to make the most of the life God had given him is remarkable.

While this story focuses much of it's telling on Robin, we mustn't forget the woman God chose to walk beside

Him. Linda is a mighty woman of God, whose strength and tenacity are most worthy. She has lived most of her married life in personal sacrifice for her husband and family. Her children can surely rise up and call her blessed; a Proverbs 31 woman indeed. She has walked out putting others first and loving out of a pure heart.

Linda's commitment to stand by her man no matter what, is commendable, and the sacrifices she was willing to make are amazing. At a time when many in this day would walk away citing it's too difficult, she remained faithful. Linda is a true woman of faith, courage, strength and love.

Even as you read the pages of her difficult journey, you don't hear complaints or excuses, but rather courage and faith. Even her fears are muffled beneath her strength and fixed focus on The Lord. She trusted God and her husband to lead and strengthen herself and her children even submitting herself to family adventures many would not dare take under "normal" circumstances. Her love overflows for her family and is evident in her service to them.

Since Robin's departure from earth it has been a delight to see Linda continue to move forward through a difficult grief process to fulfill her own destiny. I am blessed to know such a faithful, strong woman of faith. I know Robin would be so proud of his family, as am I. Thank you, Linda, for being an example of faith and courage in action and sharing your most intimate moments in this book. May God use it to bring many to Him and to strengthen countless others in the art of sacrificial giving of oneself.

I pray that as you read the pages of this book and learn about the life of one remarkable and unforgettable man of God it will challenge you to reach out to those in your sphere of influence and love them with the love of God, to never give up despite your circumstances and to keep moving forward no matter what the cost. You will be rewarded as your life reflects the saving love of Jesus Christ!

Brian Lake
Senior Pastor, Keepers of the Flame Church
& Founder, Brian Lake Ministries

TABLE OF CONTENTS

CHAPTER 1

DESIRES OF YOUR HEART

"…mom why, do you think I am still not finding the man God has for me…", "…mom do you think the man that God had for me was in an auto accident and died…", "…surely God is not expecting me to stay single for the rest of my life…."

O h, how many times as a young adult in my early twenties did I have questions like this for my mom. Many were the times the questions were also to my friends. My mom was a prayer warrior and on her knees every day, praying for me and my siblings. She was our spiritual strength and advisor over the years. Her answer to me was always encouraging. "…you know Linda, God sees the desires of your heart, and I know he has that perfect man just for you..." Together we prayed for this perfect man. She said when the time was right with God, I would meet him and he would be the man of my dreams.

It was so very hard to hear that at the time. I was living in a mindset that I was going to be an old maid for sure. I loved the Lord very much and witnessed his protection over me many times as I grew up. I learned to run to Him for my answers to life's problems. Following God's directions seemed to challenge me and would lead me through many valleys as I grew. My relationship with my earthly father was not always the best, but I knew faithfulness and living for my Heavenly Father would result in a fulfilled life. My Bible, journal and I were closely knit in those years. I sat down at one point and prayed and I decided that maybe I needed to be more specific in my prayers for a husband.

Psalms 37:4 "Delight yourself in the Lord and he will give you the desires of your heart..."

Ok....so I made my list:
1. To be a Christian man who loved the Lord.
2. For patience and understanding with a gentle spirit.
3. One who could be an example of what God would want us to be as Christians.
4. To be a leader for our children and to give them Godly encouragement.

5. And Lord if I may ask; for him to be at least 6' 2" since I am 5' 10".
6. I really like a dark complexion; it makes a man look rugged.
7. Brown hair
8. Brown eyes
9. A love for the outdoors, since I enjoy going camping.
10. And last of all, a mustache.

My list was completed and prayed over by my prayer group and me. Then it was waiting patiently in my Bible to be fulfilled.

A few months went by. Mom and Dad told me they were going camping at a nearby state park, Cowan's Gap over Memorial Day weekend in 1979. I felt God was telling me to get things right with my dad and family and I believed I needed to start listening to what God was telling me and putting the action behind it. So I planned to go along with them. I also wanted a girl's weekend out and asked Dad if I could take the camper out two weeks prior; on the weekend of May 19th and he agreed. I proceeded to make my plans with a few girlfriends.

As we registered that weekend at the camp office, the ranger behind the window seemed to be pretty good looking. As he was sitting down at the time he expressed to us girls that if we should be in need of any assistance, he would be glad to help us out. All we had to do was look him up. "Yea right, and I'll bet you say that to every female that comes to your campground". But true to his word, he made himself available often throughout that weekend.

The girls and I played some volleyball on the beach. It was too early to be swimming yet, so getting in the water was against the rules. So wouldn't you know the first minute the ball went into the water, and as I waded in after it, guess who arrived to be sure we girls were ok. "...now, girls, he said, you are not permitted in the water... If you continue I'll have to give you a citation..." Well, we became really sweet and used our female charm on him and he left us off with only the warning and he did allow us to retrieve the ball. It really was not that hard to charm someone who seemed so willing.

Latter, while boating on the lake, we heard a motor start up and low and behold a ranger pulled up on "Boat Patrol" checking to be sure we girls, and maybe the one or two other boats on the lake, had life jackets. Ok, now this was getting interesting. We walked the lake and guess who was now on "foot patrol". Yep, the same ranger. Oh, have I mentioned by now I am seeing that he is truly tall, dark and handsome. And guess what, a mustache, too! And he stood tall at 6'7".

The girls and I completed our weekend and were tearing down camp. Nearly done on a Sunday afternoon, he arrived to say goodbye and to be sure we knew that check out was at 3 pm. It was 4 pm now and he was off duty and driving a

1976 Grand Torino."...just wanted to be sure you didn't need help in tearing down camp..." Well, my heart was telling me this could be exciting. I said, "I plan to be back over the Memorial Day weekend camping with my parents, so maybe I'll see you again soon! Till then...see yah! Bye."

Two weeks later the biggest camping weekend of the season arrived. Nearly every campsite was taken and my brother and some of his friends were also camping. I got off work and tracked down my parents at their site and visited for a while. Then we went for a walk with my brother's friends. Two of these boys were standing with me when we heard this car come by and pull up..."Hey there, I've been looking for you..." Yep....one very good looking park ranger, off duty. While he went to park the car, I turned to one of the guys beside me and said, "Don't you dare leave me alone here..." It was sometime later while walking with "the ranger off duty", I found his name was Robin and as he was talking to me, I realized we were alone and no other guys were around us. I was totally taken with one Robin Reed Feight, ranger at Cowan's Gap State Park.

CHAPTER 2

ACTIVE LIFE

From the first night in the campground where we went to a movie, Beaver Valley, I knew that I had found someone with whom to share my thoughts and dreams. It may have been early, but I even thought, "This is the one who I will spend the rest of my life with." It was a funny weekend. It seemed he had brought some friends to camp with him in the park but I saw very little of them. Robin was also on duty but would come around to eat lunch with me and my parents. His donation to the boys for camping food that weekend was eggs. As he was making his rounds in the park vehicle, he tracked me down to see if I could use the eggs and cook them for his lunch. Wow….this was odd, but I enjoyed the task. Love was developed over those eggs…!

Our romance was centered around Cowan's Gap State Park the entire summer. On duty or not we found ourselves enjoying the pleasure and beauty of that park. Robin would call me and we'd meet for dinner by the lake. Just sandwiches and a drink; then he would be off to patrol the rest of the park. Sometimes I would just hang out, hoping for a glimpse of a park ranger in action. Many times I did, too. I volunteered on Sunday mornings with the Chaplain and had Sunday school class for the children camping at the park.

I lived on one side of the mountain and he lived on the other side, with the state park in the middle. It created a central location for our relationship to grow. He drove a 350 Honda motorcycle; I had a 1978 Camaro. Many of our trips back and forth across the mountain were done on that motorcycle, creating many fond memories.

Often near the end of his shift, I would get a phone call "....is it too late for me to come see you?..." No way was I turning down a visit from this handsome park ranger. So sure enough, he would come by even at 10 or 11 at night.

Shortly after we met, I found Robin in a renewed walk with the Lord. One night on his way home he called out to the Lord. Wanting to make his life right, he stopped at his church and went inside to the altar. There, he rededicated his life to God. He and I began to share in many ways spiritually. Soon, he was introducing me to some of his friends. As Christians we started meeting as a Bible study and for fellowship time. I looked over my list I had made for my heart's desires and found all ten items I could check off. In November we were engaged and on May 10, 1980 Robin and I were married. Per scripture, he now referred to me as his "rib". Oh, we were so in love, and I just knew no one was as happy as we were!

Our first home was a rented farm house. I planted flowers and made it beautiful for our life together. We were in Amish country and Robin taught me how to plant a garden and I taught him how to cook....! As the story goes, I came home from work and he was talking with a friend in our kitchen. I took a look around the kitchen observing what we might be having for dinner. Peeled potatoes cut into French fries, pot on the stove and one item plugged into the outlet on the counter. "..ummmm honey, what are we having?"

"..Well I thought I would do French fries for us..." Robin said.

Oh, that is nice, but how could I tell him, in front of our friend that he was using the popcorn popper instead of a deep fryer for the French fries. We laughed for years after that and it still comes back in our memories.

One evening I heard his motorcycle coming home and I went around the house to meet him. I smiled; he had a flat of pansies strapped down on the back rack of his motorcycle for me. He was excited as he shared a story of the laughter he received from our female Amish friends who watched him get me flowers and secure them on the bike. We laughed for a long time, and yes the flowers did survive the trip.

Many of the evenings when we were first married, Robin would work a night shift and I worked in Carlisle during the day getting home after he had left, so I would surprise him and take our dinner to the park and eat with him. Well, one day was extra special. It was his first day as the new full -time park ranger. I was so excited for him and wanted to surprise him. I arrived at the park office just as it was dusk. Lights were on inside the office and I could see two rangers talking. I stood there and stared for quite a while before I realized one was truly Robin. He was now dressed formally in a tie as was appropriate but he had shaved off his mustache and gotten his hair cut. NO WAY was this the same man I had married. But it was! I told him he was never to shave off his mustache again. I didn't like it. And he never did.

As our lives became busy with camping, hiking and loving life, we also became a part of a group called "The Crazy Christians". From church to church we did Christian Drama, even some special events outside of the churches around the area. In the summer we were involved with a coffeehouse ministry and held concerts. God was so good to us and we were happy.

Then God blessed us even more with the news of an addition to our family. Our first born, a son, Jeremy Reed arrived. But I was not the only one excited. The day after Jeremy was born, Robin left the hospital to get a bite to eat. I looked out my window in the hospital and saw him walking through the parking lot nearly skipping across the lot and every now and then he would slap the side of a light pole. Yes, he had a son and Robin was on top of the world.

So exciting and so very full now our life became. We bounced from one side of the mountain to the other sharing our joy with both sets of grandparents. One late night Robin came home from work and came up to our bedroom. Something flew by his head as he told me that there was a bat in the house. I screamed and pulled the blanket up over my head telling him to cover Jeremy in his crib. It was quiet for awhile and then I heard this swat. "...got him..." He had grabbed a tennis racket and hit the bat. He threw the bat out the window and crawled into bed laughing and very proud of what he had done.

Robin and I had been praying and decided I should be a stay at home mom. So I quit my job in Carlisle and doors opened for us to move closer to our church and Robin's home place. We were still renting but it was a beautiful new home. I learned we could live on a budget of one income by being resourceful.

Jeremy and I could sit out on our back porch and listen for his daddy to come home. Our home was on the top of a ridge and Robin would drive his motorcycle through the valley below allowing us to hear his mufflers through the trees between us. They were very loud. This became an exciting time for Jeremy and me to anticipate Robin's arrival home from work.

From the time we were married, I knew basketball was a favorite sport for Robin. He played high school and college basketball and was quite good. He also was playing in an adult league early in our relationship. One evening he and I traveled with our son back to Frederick Community College for an alumni basketball game. It was exciting seeing him on the floor and to meet his coach from college. I was proud of him. We visited with his landlady he had while going to school. Showing us all around the area and reminiscing about those college days was fun. She was so very excited to meet us and sent home with us a favorite holiday item she had made; fruit cake with rum, very heavy on the rum. We could smell it the entire way home from Frederick. Bless her heart, but it was so saturated with the rum we had to throw it away. Memories....!

Life was so wonderful, marriage being everything I dreamed it to be. We even got confirmation on additional news that I was expecting again. We practiced with Jeremy to say the word "baby" so I could have him tell my mother. It took her awhile but realized eventually what he was telling her and it made her so very happy.

Now this news began a process for building a new home. God opened the doors for us and wow, I never thought this would be possible. We started with a lot in the woods;

something we both wanted so badly. Robin ran the chain saw and cleared the property. I ran the tractor to haul the trees away. I felt like a pioneer woman. Often we would have Jeremy sit on a blanket nearby to play with his toys. As I watched him, I noticed he crawled off the blanket to a grassy area. I asked Robin to put him back and he looked at me and said "... I guess we will find out if Jeremy will be allegoric to poison"... for he was sitting right in the middle of poison ivy. What? I freaked out! But never did he get even a small bump on his body. Thank you Lord!

Our new home progressed quickly. We had a goal to be in by Sept 1, 1983 for our new baby was due shortly after. It was exciting to see each day's transformation. Finally, moving day arrived, but it was after the baby was born. On Sept 9th, our darling baby girl arrived. Elisha Mae. What a joy she brought. I had been praying for a little girl so much and praised God the minute she arrived. She was so beautiful and to a mother it formed a new bond of love. How very blessed we were, a very thankful couple, that God would give us a boy and a girl. Now too, a home we could call our own.

Thank you Father for all you have given us! We are blessed by your love.

CHAPTER 3

LOVE OF TRAVEL

I t was so very exciting to have a little girl to dress up but we did go through a time of colic. I was getting very little sleep. One night I walked into the living room where Robin was rocking his new baby girl. I held my breath at the sight I saw. Quickly, I grabbed her from his lap. He had fallen asleep and Elisha was sliding off his lap down his leg he had stretched out in front of him. Robin jumped as I reached for her, scaring her. Elisha went into crying. I took over the rocking as he went off to bed!

Robin and I were spending a lot of time involved in Crazy Christians. We acted out various skits along with our friends. They were fun and enjoyable, representing a relationship with the Father in Heaven, and the life that we desired for those around us to find the good news. John 3:16; "...For God so loved the world that he gave his only son, that whosoever believes in Him shall not perish but have eternal life…" "Crazy Christians" we were. As all of our families began to grow, the challenge for us and our friends was becoming busy. Robin really enjoyed these times as I watched him blossom into a new relationship with God. Normally, he was a quiet and rather shy man, but through these skits he began to grow spiritually and became more confident. His love for God became first in his life.

When Elisha turned two and Jeremy four in September 1985 we decided to go out to Utah to visit Robin's brother and family. We did not have much money to make this trip, but we became very creative. Adding a cap to the back of Robin's pickup, a piece of plywood, two mattress and camping supplies, we were off to see the western world. Jeremy and Elisha slept on the top mattress and Robin and I on the bottom. Jeremy and Elisha would help their daddy to drive. When we stopped for lunch, Jeremy would often challenge us while playing by the streams, both Elisha and him played and enjoyed the Colorado Mountains so very much, Yellowstone National Park, South Dakota and into Wyoming, we saw our lives unite as a family and also appreciate all that God had created. What enjoyable memories we made along the way.

We enjoyed the Glacier National Park in Montana and our visit with family living nearby. Jeremy enjoyed hiking the rocky cliffs. One morning we woke up to a glorious sunrise over huge mountain peaks of rocks. No one could ever duplicate what God had painted for us that morning. As Robin and Jeremy hiked nearby, I gathered up our things for all of us to later go for showers. Robin took Jeremy and I took Elisha. Little did we know that the showers would seem to be straight out of the mountain streams. They were not heated, and I am sure Elisha's screams could be heard throughout the entire park. I kept it as short as I could for both of us.

Visit to our family in Utah and then a return trip home. Camping along the way. It was a wonderful time together. All too soon we were traveling back home to Pennsylvania. The two weeks of travel seemed to have gone way to fast. One lasting memory of the trip was as we neared home. Stopping for gas, I came around the back of the truck and opened the passenger side door, and out of the seat something fell to the ground in front of me. I was so shocked to see Elisha face first on the cement. After tears and examination we found minor injuries on the face, Robin and I looked at each other and laughed at the way it had unfolded. Our journey was ending but would carry the memories for a lifetime.

Towards the end of October, Robin came home with plans for a one day excursion to Virginia. He would be leaving shortly for a hunting trip but wanted us to enjoy a day in the mountains while he checked out the land for a spot to hunt. While the children and I sat on a blanket with some of their toys and a picnic lunch, Robin hiked the trails above us. With his 6' 7" height his long legs made the hike look simple as we watched him go off. His excitement was high with anticipation for hunting the area once he returned and as we drove home he shared what he saw. He had even seen several of our friends from home hiking those trails.

November came and it was time for that hunting trip. My brother and friends hiked those mountains, not knowing what was about to unfold in the few days ahead. Robin returned to me and the children on the 19th of November in 1985 unsuccessful but full of life and a huge story of the "big" one that got away!

He still was on leave, so we decided on November 20, 1985 to make a choice that would change our life and our destiny for the rest of our lives.........

I John 4:4; "...greater is He who is in you than He that is in the world..."

CHAPTER 4

A CHANGE IN LIFE'S GOALS

November 20, 1985 was a sunny warm day for November. It was a great day for cutting firewood and taking the children along into the mountains. The tractor was parked and Robin and his father went in the direction to cut trees. I took the children and started up the mountain where my tree stand was set up for deer season. I heard the saw and heard trees falling.

Moments later I heard Robin's dad screaming for me to come quickly. My first thoughts were a chainsaw cut and Robin was bleeding. I sat the children near the tractor and told them to stay there. I prayed, "Dear Lord help us with whatever is ahead". Dad was saying to me he was going for help as I got near to Robin who was on the ground. There was no blood that I could see and Robin looked at me and said, "Well this is going to ruin a good day for cutting fire-wood." As it would turn out it would be more than a day.

As Robin and I sat there waiting for help I heard a tractor trying to start. Looking up, I realized that Jeremy, at age four was in the seat and trying to get it started. I panicked, "...Lord help us..." I ran to him and Elisha and planted them on the ground and gave them strict orders to not move and I took the key. When I ran back to Robin, he and I prayed together. We knew he could not move his legs; his arms were moving though somehow not just right. "Father we know that you have this in your control; please keep us in your protective arms." I was scared!

Robin was unable to hold his arms up on his own and I was concerned to try and move him. I told him to be still till help arrived. He had a lump on the back of his head that ached but that was the only visible injury. I tried to reach under his head and dig out some dirt to relieve some pressure to the area where the lump was. It seemed to take a long time before help arrived. But our local fire department arrived and they were wonderful. Dad came up with them and he went to the children and started down the mountain with them. After assessing the injuries the EMTs placed Robin on a backboard. Then he was lifted into the back of a neighbor's four-wheel drive pickup that had a layer of corn freshly picked from the field. We tried to keep him balanced but it was nearly impossible. Wading the creek was even harder.

Finally arriving at the house, the ambulance was waiting for us. They allowed me to ride in the front as we headed to the local medical center emergency room. They stabilized Robin and took x-rays. I thought him to be OK, nothing out of the ordinary until they told us they were transferring us to Chambersburg Hospital. I was still not realizing the severity of Robin's injuries. I remember thinking this will be OK. I have family in Chambersburg and I can stay with them while Robin is in the hospital. As we were going down the mountain on Route 30 towards Chambersburg Hospital, Robin called for me through the opening to the front where I sat. "Honey...did I put on clean underwear this morning..."? I looked at our driver and we both started to laugh and then we both stopped and looked at each other, not sure of how we should be reacting, the unknown of what was taking place, but even then Robin's humor was evident in the midst of a bad circumstance.

Arrival at Chambersburg Hospital was a scurry of activities as doctors and nurses were given orders right and left. I was in the hallway when the doctor came to me and said, "...your husband's neck is dislocated between cervical 6 and 7."

Ok, what does this mean?

"...Mrs. Feight I am sorry to say your husband will never walk again..." They also told me we were transferring to Hershey Medical Center.

What a blow....It took me sometime to process all this as he walked away leaving me there. How could he be so insensitive? Robin's mom and dad drove to Chambersburg and all I could say was they were transferring him to Hershey. I am not sure what else I said. But it wasn't long before they left to start the journey to Hershey. As we loaded Robin and continued on to our next destination, I became very quiet and prayed the entire trip. I was very thankful that I was allowed to be in the ambulance with Robin. I prayed for our journey that may lie ahead; for God's divine intervention, for Chambersburg's diagnosis to be wrong, and for me to be strong. Going to Hershey to me at that moment meant things were serious. We arrived at the ER and the scurry of activity began all over again.

I was sent to the waiting room until a nurse came out to get me. I was allowed to be with him the entire time. A doctor came in and explained in more detail Robin's injury and what had happened. The vertebras separated and slid out of place pinching the spinal cord. I remember him making a comment to Robin, "...there is more to life than any thought of using a gun..." It took me days to realize he was trying to see just what thoughts were going through Robin's head and how he was about to handle being paralyzed. Robin was quick to tell him he believed he would one day walk again and life was given by God and he had no intentions to end it by using a gun. The doctor looked at him, then at me, nodded and walked away.

The staff explained to us what was to happen next. A halo vest was to be placed on Robin's head and then he would be sent up to the ICU. While this was taking place, I had to leave the room so I went to the waiting room and totally lost control of my emotions. Processing and trying to make sense out of all the information given to us in the last hours of this day, I felt it was more than I could do to stay in the room to watch as they drilled into his scull for placement of the halo vest. This was my husband, my love, and he was going to have a long challenge ahead.

I got myself under control and returned to the room. They now had him in a halo and were adjusting an extra exten-sion to the bottom of Robin's bed. "...Honey, the beds here are too short..." "... They have to add a piece just for me..." Smiling at him we caught each other's eyes. Now that he was flat the way they wanted him, we went to the elevator to go up to ICU. The nurse directed me to stand by Robin's head and I was holding his hand talking to him when we both realized there was an issue. He did not fit in the elevator and the staff was clueless on what to do next. "...Honey this ele-vator isn't big enough for us tall men such as myself..." "... OK, guys this is what we'll do..." '...bend my legs at the knees to the one side...remove the extension on the bed and hit the up button..." I had to laugh with him as they seem to process what Robin was saying. We did do just as he suggested.

We arrived at the floor needed and we found ourselves in ICU. Time seemed to move all too slowly. The nurses were sure he was stable and said I was to go home and get some sleep. I took a look at myself and realized I was in an old tee shirt and torn jeans from being in the woods to cut firewood. I turned to Robin in tears and said I did not want to leave him. In walked our pastors...really at the time they were friends...one did become a pastor later. I knew as we all prayed together that Robin was now in God's hands and those of our dear friends. Mom and Dad Feight spent some time with goodbyes and I kissed him and hugged him the best I could saying I would be back in a few hours. His parents and I then left for home.

Walking into our house alone that night, I dropped to my knees and cried and prayed. I did not know what to do next. Life as we knew it would never be the same. Married for five years and two children...God help me walk through this!

CHAPTER 5

STRUGGLES DAY BY DAY

I don't know that I really slept any that night. But I got up and packed clothes for Jeremy and Elisha for an extended stay with my parents. I packed myself some things and took off for my parent's home to see my children. I knew they were so young. How would I explain to them what had happened to their daddy and the changes in our lives? When I got there I just held them tightly, and told them how very much I loved them. Their daddy would not be home for a while and we would need to pray for him every day. My mom and dad said they would do anything to help. At this time it was to watch our children.

When I arrived at Hershey and went straight to ICU, I stopped totally in my tracks when I found Robin not there where I had left him. I was dazed and scared and my heart seemed to sink. When a nurse found me and said they had moved him to a room, my emotions rolled on. When I found him he had a smile for me and we prayed together for God to walk us step by step. I remember Robin had oxygen on which was forming ice cycles on his mustache and beard. He was shivering and cold. I spent the nights in the waiting room sleeping on a love seat. I was allowed to go in at any time for short periods of time. When he was awake we'd talk about the children, what we wanted to do with our new home we had just built, and how we wanted to landscape it once we got home. We talked about God's directions too and where we might be heading in the days or months ahead keeping a positive attitude the best we could!

One day the doctor came in to say they were going to do surgery on his neck. He had to line up the vertebrae and then wire it so it would fuse together properly. I prayed really hard as did many others. I guess I was believing in a miracle that once the spinal column was lined up, it would permit the spinal fluid to go through the section that was crushed and allow movement to return as well as the ability to move his limbs.

As per the doctor, surgery was successful. As for me, it was not the miracle I was praying for. But Father God, let me be a light and shine for you in all of this.

Isaiah 41:10; "...fear not, for I am with you; be not dismayed, for I am your God; I will strengthen you, I will help you. I will up hold you with my righteous right hand.

In the days that followed we would put a sheep skin over the vest on Robin's chest so that Elisha could nap on daddy. Jeremy said very little. I am not sure what he understood. He was my little man and I tried to share my heart with him while we played with some toys in the waiting room. The children did not come down often while we were in Hershey Medical Center. It was an hour and a half drive so they stayed with Robin's parents or mine.

While recovering from the surgery, Robin was placed in a bed that rotated ever so slowly from side to side to help with pressure points. I'd sit on one side for a bit then jump up and go to the other side in order to talk with him. It became a time of laughter for us. Hershey, being a teaching institute, gave Robin every opportunity to be used as a training tool. He loved it, but I got so tired of every team picking and prodding him on his feet and legs. I finally told Robin it needed to stop. Robin's response was, "...How will they ever learn if they don't use me?..." Well, I didn't care; try it on someone else's husband. He carried those scars with him his entire life on the bottom of his feet.

We finally went to a standard room and Robin in his bed was longer than the width of the room. The nurse and I tried to move his bed one day so we could put his head in the small sink to wash his hair. What a mess. I think we got the bed stuck at one point. Remember also there is still a three foot extension on the end for his feet, but we did eventually get clean hair.

By now a week had gone by. I had slipped home overnight to check on the house and children and to repack. We had the grandparents taking turns; one week each watching the children. I was trying so hard to get as much normal into their lives as possible.

As I went back to Robin, it was on Thanksgiving Day. I walked into his room to find him with tears running down his face. When I asked him what was wrong. He said, "...I got turkey..." All he had been praying for was mashed potatoes and gravy for Thanksgiving. Up to this day he had no solids. But here he was thanking the Lord for turkey, stuffing and cranberry sauce. I cried with him. We learned to be thankful for every step forward in the days to follow.

A few days later we received the word that Robin was being transferred to a spinal cord rehab. It was now December, so as we approached the facility, I saw lots of trees, dead with no leaves, cold and snow. The very old buildings had bars on the windows. At one time this was used as a state hospital. I was immediately depressed by our surroundings.

Robin was taken inside and I was greeted by someone giving me instructions to go to the Admissions Office. I was to take the elevator to the bottom floor, and follow the footsteps from there. I got into the elevator and hit the lowest number which said basement. The doors opened and I saw the footsteps I was to follow. The walls were black, the ceiling low with pipes hanging from the top. I cried out to God, "Why are we in this place?"

The footsteps led me into a clinic area for returning patients. This was more cheerful and appeared to be largely for children. I told the receptionist why I was there and she took me to the Admissions Office and proceeded to explain what would take place. We would likely be here for five to six months and most likely my insurance, state insurance, would not cover the cost. We were looking at the cost of $300,000 to $500,000 in expenses. So I might as well figure on declaring bankruptcy and face the fact that I would lose our home.

I was devastated. How cruel and unprofessional these people were! I cried as I left their office to follow footsteps back to the elevator. I stopped myself but I continued to cry. How could we ever survive? I prayed, "Lord, help me make sense of all this please." I knew I had to make some phone calls but for now I needed to be strong, go up this elevator and smile for Robin, to be an encourager. And that is exactly what I did. We were placed in a very small room with three other men. They had Robin in his bed and took care of all their questions for him by the nurse and aids who would be caring for him. They gave me a list of items he would need. High top sneakers, to keep his ankles and feet lined up, sweat pants for easy on/off during rehab exercises, etc. So this is what it was to be like for five months.

At one point, I was visited by a social worker who made arrangements for me to stay in one of the onsite housing facilities, a large dorm of different size rooms with shared bathrooms. Mine was a small bedroom with two double beds that had the old iron frames. It did serve the purpose, and I was thankful for it. It provided a way to for me to be nearby for Robin. It also allowed me to bring the children down occasionally to visit with Robin through the week. And I would have them sleep in the extra bed in my room.

The first few days, Robin remained in his bed and we pushed him down to rehab in it. They gave him weights on his wrists to try and build up his arm muscles. We tried to look for positive things. Many children were around us and I would tell Robin of their circumstances. Some were brain injuries. Robin wasn't able to move very much in his bed unless we would turn him. We became very emotional at seeing some of the children. And yet we became thankful for Robin not having any brain damage. That tree limb was really close to his head.

After getting into a routine, they began to "train" his body. It brought a new knowledge to him and me. Our roommates soon became our friends and fellow survivors with us. One was a single Mennonite guy, one a husband whose wife also was staying near me in the housing. The third was a young man who made life for the nurses a challenge. Let's just say he enjoyed his weekend's home too much. And he had no family support to help him with his care. We fell into a routine each day.

Before we knew it Christmas was nearly here. How does one celebrate with two small children in a rehab? "...Jesus is the Reason for the Season..." so we will remember this! And continue on........

CHAPTER 6

MAKING IT THE BEST IN A BAD SITUATION

On Christmas Day the staff allowed us to have the dining room in the afternoon. There was a fake Christmas tree in the corner. Robin was in his bed and we wheeled him down to the room. Both sides of our family came together. We exchanged gifts mainly for the children, Jeremy and Elisha. And as family goes, we had lots of food to go around. Yes there were those at times who grabbed a corner for a good cry, but we came back together for as much cheer as we could bring to make the best of a bad situation.

Robin was pleased that most of the food was based on his favorites. I was just very thankful and grateful for all those who came to brighten our day.

My last memory that Christmas Day was my brother taking the last two guests home with him. I waved goodbye as Jeremy and Elisha disappeared with him down the road. I turned and left my tears freely flow. My heart was so broken and torn. God, please help me! As I made my way back to my husband, I felt exhausted and still knew I needed to spend some time saying goodnight to him and get him ready for bed. I later would allow myself to cry freely in my room till I would fall asleep.

As the week continued through our everyday routine, Robin began experiencing shortness of breath and told the nurses he felt like an elephant was sitting on his chest. We were not sure what was going on with this. Robin would shiver and shake for hours in the evening. They found him to have what they called "drug fever". Changing his meds did seem to help with this, but we were still having an issue with the breathing.

Shortly after I arrived one morning, I was to find they were sending Robin back to Hershey. We had a nice rehab nurse who was going to go along in the ambulance while I followed in the car. At Hershey we found there were pulmonary emboli in his lungs which are basically small blood clots.

It became touch and go for a while. I didn't want to leave Robin, so I would stay as long in his room as I could and get away with it, and then moved to the waiting room to sleep on a chair there. Finally, I was kicked out of there by security, crying as I left the hospital, not sure what was going to happen till I returned. I went to a nearby hotel for a couple hours till daybreak and then came back. They told me his protein level was very low and desperately needed him to eat. But every time I tried to sneak meat with mashed potatoes or gravy, Robin would get irritated with me. They would take me aside and say he could die. I finally broke down in front of Robin and pleaded with him to eat.

At this point he had a vision that he would share for years to come. As it unfolded Robin saw to the bottom of a dry hand dug well, but at the very bottom in a small pool of water were the words, "...Let the Weak say I am Strong...." As Robin saw these words, God impressed him to speak them out loud, which he obeyed. The more he said them the stronger he became. God revealed to him that this was a point of life and death for him. I, too, believe this for I began to see a new strength in Robin. Thank you Lord!

I also believe that God gave wisdom to the nurses as they began to feed Robin protein milk shakes.

This was the second time that God had given Robin a vision while in Hershey. During the initial admission, Robin was asleep and God woke him up in his spirit and had him looking out his doorway of his room. Through the hall came a fighter jet and as it got to him, he was immediately swooped up into the jet. Flying through the halls of the hospital it took a dive to the left and at the end of the hall were plate glass windows. The jet flew through the glass and into the outside. As Robin looked back he saw the front of the

Hershey Medical Center. In front of him he saw mountain peaks, some low some high. Every so often it got narrow for the passages. Approaching one pass, he knew they would not make it through. The jet fired missiles, hitting the target and opening up the passage. He continued through like this for awhile and returned to the hospital through the glass windows, down the hall to his room. When he woke up, he was in his bed, able for the first time in the weeks after the accident to take a deep breath, Colorado clear air as he called it. Robin explained the vision as though he were flying through his spinal column and as they approached the area that was out of place he felt he witnessed God removing the blockage of those areas that were hindering him for breathing. Also, his hands became more limber and allowing him more use.....

Back now in the Hershey Medical Center we saw Robin improving but they would not allow us to go back to the rehab. We knew the longer we stayed away from the rehab our time would be extended for his recovery. We just wanted to get home. During this time we discovered the rehab nurses and staff had gone on strike. OK, so just let us go home. The time for Robin to have his Halo vest removed had come. So while at Hershey we were happy to see this take place. Now we felt there was no reason why I could not take him home. The doctor at Hershey agreed and was about to do so. I had already been doing most of Robin's care anyway. However, we got a solid stop sign from the rehab. It seemed that if we left we would not be able to come back to the rehab. We had to complete their process the way they wanted it to be. Robin and I were both very homesick. I broke down in tears, and the rehab staff saw I was at the end of my rope. I had a meltdown in front of them. It was only a couple days and we were back at the rehab.

Wow, did things change quickly. Robin had been in a wheel chair at times, but now they became more often and they allowed us a first outing. Learning how to transfer in and out of a car and how to maneuver were hard for Robin in his chair because he was still so weak. But he worked hard and became stronger to do his transfers. The weekend came and we had two of our faithful friends come and go with us to a local restaurant.

These two friends had been so supportive and faithful. Every Thursday night they would come to the rehab and the four of us met in the chapel and prayed and laughed and just fellowshipped. But this night we were going off campus to a restaurant. Our first order of business was to get Robin transferred into a car. Being 6'7" only allowed the challenge to become belly laughing hilarious. Once the legs were in and Robin's head was not. He was laughing so hard no one but me seemed to be so scared they would actually hurt him. Our trip was full of the same laughter. Even trying to get him out of the car and back into the wheelchair to go into the restaurant had us once more in hysterical laughter. What a wonderful evening we had. We found it to be a beginning that life truly could go on and we were going to be fine.

Occasionally, I started to bring Jeremy and Elisha down to spend a few days with me in my room so Robin would also have time with his children. It took no time at all for Jeremy to find a toy room nearby that was for the children's ward. They allowed our children to play there also. So our new life was a challenge but doable.

Throughout this time I had been in contact with different people and learned that truly we did have fairly good insurance and our coverage would be about 80 per cent of all our bills. So now I was relieved but did not have a clue as to what the 20 percent would be that I would have to pay. I have totally depended on the Lord so far and I knew he would open the doors to help us in some way. Many were the cards we received with monetary gifts that allowed for expenses to be met during the rehab time. I stashed away much of the money for what might lie ahead.

March held open doors for us to buy a van. I had a Camaro and there was no way I was getting Robin and his 6'7" frame in and out of it for transfers. Nor could I get two children in plus wheelchair and diaper bags. We depended on others and their vehicles to get us home for visits and outings on the weekends during this time.

So off I went in search of a van. On March 21, 1986 we picked up a van with a lift installed. Only by the monetary gifts was the lift paid for in full. I had no idea what God had in store for paying for the van itself. We drove the van to the rehab at the end of our weekend visit home. It was Robin's 30th birthday, also. So as a special treat and gift, we engaged our friends from home to have a party and a Christian concert with the "Sweet Freedom" band, held in the auditorium for all of those in the rehab.

Only a few weeks later, five months from the day we entered the rehab, we were told discharge was available. Halleluiah! With this also brought a scary time for me. Could I do this and take care of two young children? Both of us shed tears as we left the rehab campus that day.

It was bittersweet; glad to leave but now a new challenge lay ahead. New beginnings! Dear Jesus we need you more than ever. Direct our paths as you promised please guide us and give me the strength in all things that lie ahead.

I Chronicles 16:11; "...Seek the Lord and His strength; seek His presence continually..."

CHAPTER 7

CHALLENGES

HOME:

"...a residence, dwelling, habitat. A place where a person feels he/she belongs. Family that lives together, the familiar of security. Comfort and love by family together in one location..."(1)

Here we were, full of love for each other. Daddy's little girl who could do no wrong, a son who was to be just like daddy when he grows up, and a wife who would love him until we were old and gray. A husband to forever be by my side as we walked out the life God had placed before us.

The challenges were set before us. One day at a time, Sweet Jesus, one day at a time. My morning would begin sometimes at 5:30 a.m. and end at midnight. It took a while to develop some kind of routine and to find if there could be any "normal."

On our first day home, Robin was my first priority. We would get his personal care and needs completed, dress and be ready to meet the day. Now, to get from the bed to his wheelchair, I would take off the arm rests; slide his legs out across his seat. Then he would grab my arms and we would pull him up into a sitting position. I then took hold behind his knees and pivot him to face the front. Replacing the arm rests and foot pegs. I would then push him to the sink in the kitchen so we could wash his hair and dry it. He then proceeded to brush his teeth and use his electric razor for shaving. This was all in the span of about two hours.

By now the children were awake. Elisha would climb up on her daddy's lap and I got breakfast for everyone. Robin would talk with each of the children; Jeremy about his Tonka trucks, or what he might build in the sandbox outside and what outfit Elisha might wear on her doll baby that day. My thoughts were to get breakfast over, do the dishes, make up the beds, get the children dressed, and start a load of laundry.

Robin's personal needs would then need to be cared for. I would switch the laundry, decide what I would get out of the freezer for dinner, talk to the children about keeping a path for daddy to get through the toys, and I needed to rearrange furniture so Robin could maneuver the best he could through the house. As I finished re-arranging furniture and folded laundry, it was time for lunch, so once more I did dishes, cleaned up and went back to finishing preparations for dinner, or, doing more of the laundry while trying to run the sweeper or mop the kitchen. I went to help Robin once more, and then to be there for Jeremy or Elisha when needing me throughout the day. At dinner, we tried to enjoy it together as a family at the table. Then there was the clean-up and baths for both children. We shared an evening Bible story together and prayer, gave kisses and the children were off to bed. I then reversed the process for Robin as I got him into bed, undressed him and took care of his needs. Afterwards, I took my shower, dressed for bed and set my alarm as I looked at the clock at 11 pm. One day in! I reached over to give Robin a kiss and hug and told him I loved him. We cried together and he kissed me, totally aware of what my day had become. This is what it was to be like as we took each day one at a time here after.

We soon discovered our needs were for an easier entrance to get into the house. Friends had made us some ramps. But we lived on a hill and the front was all grass. So it was hard to wheel Robin up and down the yard by myself, making our trips away limited. After discussing some options, we made arrangements for a patio to be put on the back of our house as soon as possible and put in a patio door off the kitchen. We extended the driveway to the back of the house where a ramp came off the patio to the van. Thanks to many helpers and friends, it made our life so much easier and Robin now had the ability to be outside.

CHAPTER 8

LIFE LESSONS

R obin and I recognized the need for him to become stronger. If he could lift himself up then he could do transfers. We checked out a local exercise room. So at least two or three days a week I would load him and the children into the van and go to McConnellsburg. At first the instructor and I had to assist him but as he slowly became stronger he was able to do more for himself.

For a Quadriplegic (C-6/C-7) Robin did become very strong. He built up to lifting 40 pounds or more, and he could see the difference at home as we would do transfers from wheelchair to bed. And eventually he figured out ways to dress himself. By using his thumbs he could hook them in the belt loops of his pants and roll from side to side on the bed pulling his pants up. Keeping his shirts buttoned, all but two on top, he would pull them over his head. Again by rolling from side to side, he tucked in the shirt tail. We learned as we went. Buying Robin's shoes in an extra size larger than size 13 helped him, but trying to find a size 14 was really hard.

One area that bothered him was watching me mow our lawn. He would sit on the front porch with his mind turning out solutions. "…you know Linda, if I would get a tractor, a John Deere tractor, with hydraulics, I know I could mow the lawn…" Sure honey, that's all we needed, was for you to roll a tractor down our very steep front embankment.

By the following summer, a friend showed up with an automatic John Deere tractor with hydraulics. Every time Robin's mind would speak out his thoughts, God would use someone to show up! And he not only mowed our lawn but many in the neighborhood for years to come!

As winter approached, Robin became just a little distant, looking at his own issues and not feeling really happy. God knew what he needed. God told Robin to get his eyes off himself and see what he could do for someone else. So he began to pray! Along came a friend who suggested to Robin that maybe he could substitute teach at our local school. Unsure of this, he questioned what he could possibly bring to the kids while being in a wheelchair. Also, Robin had a learning disability of his own while in school growing up. What would the teachers think of him? Many knew of his struggles he had while in school. Well, he'd give it a try to see if they would even consider him at the school. It worked. Over the years ahead he would become one of the favored substitutes for the teachers at the school. He operated under his favorite scripture verse,

Philippians 4:13 "...I can do all things through Christ who strengthens me..."

I was thrilled for him, but this meant I had to rise early to get him dressed. Dressing the children and loading everyone into the van and taking daddy to "work" was a challenge. Jeremy was just starting kindergarten, so I was able to drop him off along the way, also. Elisha and I would hold down the home front. She was so great at entertaining herself for which I thanked God often. I would get caught up in cleaning and/or laundry and realize she was missing. But after a quick search, I would find her playing with her baby dolls in her room and making dinner on her kitchen set. In the afternoon, she and I would get into the van and go pick up daddy and Jeremy at the school. It worked and everyone seemed to be happy with our new normal.

Being at the school Robin became a little more confident in himself which was a good thing, and God was the only one who knew what was to lie ahead. Robin was presented once more with another challenge. The Jr. High Boys Basketball team was in need of an assistant coach. OK, what could a man who was a good basketball player but now in a wheelchair, have to offer these boys? We both needed to pray about this one, for I would need to drive him. I was all for Robin being as active as he could be. He was depending more and more on the Lord and growing spiritually. We even opened our home for Bible studies. I was fortunate to be a stay at home mom and had the ability to also be his caregiver. So what would being a coach bring to us? I said yes to helping him and he agreed we'd give it a try. The home games went fairly well; the away games were more challenging. I had to drive him in the van to these because he was unable to get on the bus.

I began to see a pattern take place. A meek, rather shy 6'7" man became confident in himself and his ability to share his knowledge of basketball. As he put more of himself into the students, he also developed a relationship with them. Robin had a way with the boys on the team to give them positive encouragement. He also watched out for them in the classroom as well, trying to keep them on task with school work. During the basketball season, I would often see him in a huddle with an arm around someone's shoulder and going over a play.

At one practice he asked me to help him with a lesson he wanted to give to the boys. Over Robin's career in playing basketball he had gained quite a collection of trophies. We loaded them all on a cart and covered them and placed them in a room behind the gym ... all but one, a small trophy, but one that was most significant to Robin. He sat the boys down at practice and started to share with them about the choices they would make in their future and how he prayed that they would make good ones. He also explained to the boys that only their faith in God could give them the strength and abilities to make those right choices. As he continued, he shared with them the story of one high school game that became very important to him. He was so determined to play well enough in this game that he could bring home a trophy. That's all he wanted was one trophy. Well not only did he play well in that game, but he succeeded in bringing home a trophy; not just any trophy, but the "MVP", most valuable player trophy. At this point he proudly showed his team this one small trophy. But the boys did not seem all that impressed. As he continued with the life lesson of perseverance and determination, he asked Jeremy to bring out the cart behind the gym. There, on that cart, were displayed various trophies of Robins' successful years of playing basketball while in high school and some larger ones from playing college basketball at Frederick Community College. Some he received while play on an adult league too. Continuing into the Life's Lesson, he said,"... Today, in a wheelchair, everyday still becomes a choice of determination to succeed in whatever I put my hands to do..." I was so very proud of my husband and how he overcame his many challenges.

But that day will stand out to me, as a time when I have never been more proud of the man I had married and what we, together as a family, were to accomplish in the lives of these students.

Over the years our home would be opened to these boys as they looked to Robin for his life lessons. Sometimes they would work hard together, but then there were the rewards of the fun outings he would plan for them. He encouraged them and gave them the positive outlook so many of them needed. The very night that the season came to an end and we were leaving the parking lot of the school, he said to me, "…Linda, if I would get hand controls for this van, I know I could drive it…" Yes Robin, I am sure you could. We had them installed shortly after. Taking one practice run after school in their parking lot, he drove me home. It was very rare after that that he allowed me to drive his van when he/we had to go somewhere.

CHAPTER 9

NEW LIFE CHALLENGES

With Robin's "independence" now as a driver, nothing seemed to stand in his way. He drove the Amish from Spring Run to Lancaster and Philadelphia. That really was an experience. Elisha would often go along with her daddy. Each stop at an Amish farm produces someone who was going along. Soon the van would be full. Some sat on lawn chairs. Today, that would never happen. Always, Robin and Elisha were well fed. Whether it was a wedding, funeral or doctor appointment, good Amish cooking prevailed. Once I smiled when Elisha came home. Trying to be polite, she said; "...mommy, they did not smell too nice in the van today..." I took this time as a life lesson and explained to Elisha how the Amish were a very hard working community. And they loved God very much. But a lot of their day is taking care of the animals in the barn. And the various smells from the barn stay with them throughout the day. Just like pappy Reed's barn and animals are.

We loved to camp, so one weekend we packed up the van with a tent and supplies. We traveled to a nearby campground and began to unload. The children so enjoyed this time. It was a tremendous amount of work for me but I was striving to keep our lives as normal and enjoyable as I could so I did my best. I took the children on a hike, and because it was uphill Robin stayed behind by our camp fire. We had not gone very far up the road when there was a very loud explosion. Jeremy said. "...Mommy that's from our campsite..." I agreed and we ran back as quickly as we could.

There sat Robin bent over with laughter. His wheel on his manual wheelchair had exploded. He was just a little too close to the fire. "...You think it was loud where you were at? You should have been sitting here..." We loaded him in the van and headed to the nearest bike shop for a new tire. We also bought a spare to keep in the van, just in case it was needed in the future.

During this same camping trip, I was informed that there was a wheelchair lift by the in ground pool that we could use. So I threw Robin in the pool so he could swim with the children and me. He loved to swim and even though paralyzed, he floated. We all had a wonderful time. Robin started to get cold and honestly, he was looking a little shriveled from being in so long. So I went in search of the lifeguard to run the lift in order to get him out of the pool. No way....! I was now informed there is no one that could operate the lift, nor did anyone know where the key even was. We slowly worked our way up the steps on the shallow edge of the pool. With none of the lifeguards offering to help, Robin and I tried to lift up over the edge of the pool. Success, but how was I to get him into his wheel chair. I pulled over a lawn chair that was the old tri-folds. By now he was shivering so badly, and I was near tears. He lifted as much as he could while I pulled on the back of his swimming trunks. Finally, from the lawn chair and into his wheelchair we made it. I wrapped him in every beach towel I had along. I placed Elisha on his lap, gave Jeremy the beach bag and together we pushed and pulled our way to the van and back to camp. We quickly did change of clothing and wrapped him in sweatshirts and hoodies to get Robin's temperature warmed up.

We did enjoy our evening camping by the fire and our last night's stay in the tent. This, too, was a challenge, getting Robin from his wheelchair down to the air mattress on the floor of the tent. Morning came and we headed for home after loading our gear. Wow...was it nice to be home! Now I started the unloading of our gear and putting it all away. I don't know who was more tired than I that night, but Robin and the children came to me and said, Thank you for such a nice time of camping! Suddenly, all the tiredness went away. It was a good weekend because we were together as a family. And I would and did do more camping trips in the years ahead but just not in a tent ever again! We were able later to purchase a used tag along camper which was more comfortable.

After our camping trip, Robin decided it was time to get an electric wheelchair. Robin did do well in his manual chair on flat surfaces, but soon found his limits because he was such a high level injury and because he was so tall, I found I was pushing him more and more. I made him promise not to become lazy... ha ha ha!

Once he got his electric wheelchair and the van adapted for him, it gave Robin much more freedom. Now he, alone, would take off and go to school for substituting and coaching boys' basketball. And now with a John Deere tractor and a trailer to haul it, he was off to the mountains, to valleys, where ever Robin wanted to go he took some mode of transportation. He explored places where one would take only an ATV. There were those incidents, such as one of a meadow that was too wet, and he sunk in to his axles! Thank goodness for neighbors with tractors to pull him out of the tight spots.

As Elisha grew older, she went off to school, and Robin now had his freedom. It allowed me to go back into the work force. So life really became busier. I planned an organized my days continually. From sun up to sun down, my mind was constantly planning; many of my well organized days were changed at a moment's notice by a suggestion from Robin.

A memory on one occasion while at home, was of him exploring a trail in the woods beside our property. I was standing in the kitchen doing dishes and a very emotional little girl came running in crying. She was so upset that it took me awhile to make sense of anything she was saying. She did not appear to be hurt, but Daddy was somewhere. She took my hand and we ran for the woods. I rounded the corner of our house and I could see the wheelchair upside down and Robin on the ground. I could hear him saying, "...Is Elisha ok? Is Elisha ok?" I assured him she was; then looked at him. He, too, seemed to be fine. When I asked what happened, he said Elisha was riding on the back of his wheelchair and they were exploring together when he hit a hole, causing him to upset backwards with Elisha on it...!

"...and what did we learn from this? I asked Robin...?"

"...He said, "Not to hit a hole while Elisha was riding on the back..." of course, with a huge smile on his face.

My how wonderful! My thoughts were, "...Robin let's not ride the wheelchair through the woods again..." But, of course, that would never happen with his adventurous spirit.

He took that wheelchair more places in the woods than one should ever venture. So next on the list was to take the John Deere tractor to the woods. This opened a whole new door to opportunity; adventures for a lifetime of enjoyment with a few scars along the way. Having the tractor allowed for mowing every opportunity that he could, for friends and neighbors during sickness, or just because he could. It was some way for him to give back to his community. Those in the area remember many times that Robin would drive on the berm of the road from one location to another. Even the friend who supplied the John Deere tractor knew him well enough to include a flashing yellow marker light on the back.

To drive the van was an honor he would display to so many. From airport pick-ups for conferences, to family outings or vacations with his family, it made him feel important and blessed to be able to do what came natural for him and that was to be a servant to so many in so many ways. Many times in their travels, Robin became the tour guide and educated those passengers on the history of the area. Each adventure, whether with family or friend, a trip with Robin was always a memorable one.

Hunting became such a great pleasure and enjoyment. Friends enjoyed the times spent putting on drives or seeing Robin's success in shooting a deer, turkey or just a rabbit. He was always happy with those around him who would have success even if he had not. Many were the friends over the years that would enjoy time with Robin in the mountains. And many were the tall tale stories that came out of those experiences, from the big one that got away, to the funnel cake shack that was created to keep them warm and supplied with good fellowship.

There was a late summer day, while at the farm, when the family was scattered outside doing different things. When one of us heard something, I listened and said that it was Robin hollering from the mountain. Well, it seemed he was stuck on a tree stump and could not get loose while riding his John Deere tractor and mowing for hunting season. A rescue had to take place by family. He thought it to be fun; I thought it to be a lesson for the future.

On another occasion for a hunting story was while on his John Deere tractor during turkey season. Many of us knew he was in the woods, but as it got dark and we did not see him come in, we became concerned. Thanks to a nearby neighbor who was out feeding his dogs, and heard what he thought were hunters off in the distance, he stopped to listen long enough to the hollering and shooting, it turned out to be Robin stuck in the mud in a creek. He was trying for a very long time to get someone's attention and it was getting darker. He was cold and running low on ammo that he had been shooting to get someone's attention. He even scared himself this time. Within a few days we purchased our first cell phone and he promised to never again go somewhere without telling someone where he was hunting.

He loved to make plans for the young adults to experience life. With the help of some friends, Robin would plan to pick up and delivery these boys to a designated spot in the woods along a creek. With no electric or modern conveniences, this

"He Man" camp enjoyed an entire weekend of activities in the woods. Those boys will always have those memories.

Robin planned canoe trips. Borrowing canoes from a friend, the children and the canoes were taken to the lake where each young person had to prove himself or herself in the operations of a canoe. Safety was always first with Robin. Though he was unable to go out in the canoes himself, he observed from the shoreline to be confident they were doing what needed to be done. No free rides were given. They had to unload and reload the canoes on the trailer, and to make sure each one had a life vest. Once everyone passed the test, the reward followed. He would take them to a location along a creek and they would unload the canoes for floating. Making sure each one was safe, Robin knew very well where he could drive along the route and observe the canoes as they floated down. The adults who went along also benefited in the pleasure of nature and the peacefulness of floating a canoe down the creek. When they would reach their destination, Robin was there to pick them up with a huge smile on his face as each one shared excitement of the trip.

Our children grew up with history stories from Robin while riding in the van. History was another of his loves. Our trips were always memorable with a cooler full of snacks, cheese, bologna, grapes and strawberries. As they have grown older, it has become a time of laughter and remembrance of those snacks. But it made it possible for a family on a budget to still enjoy traveling. More than once, though, there were frustrations in our travels, as the van lift would go down, get stuck with Robin on it, and not go back up. But God would always provide someone to help us. Often, Robin, himself, would talk us through the steps and get us back in working order, or, we improvised with a bungee cord to keep the doors closed until we found someone who could help us.

Family outings with our camper also brought us enjoyment. As the children were now older, they were able to help me load the supplies for our weekend getaways. But it was still somewhat challenging when the time came to go to bed. I would transfer Robin into the camper through the door onto to floor. Then the children each took a foot and me the back of his pants, sliding him to our bed in the back portion of the camper. Then we would turn him over on his knees and step by step up onto the bed. Now this was all in a hallway that was may be two feet wide. We learned later as we went camping that it was easier to just put a mattress on the floor in front of the doorway and that's where he would sleep for the night. Early in the morning he was the first one that I would get out of the camper.

One memory of a camping trip was a time I nearly poisoned Robin. It's funny today but at the time it was not. I had made French toast. I sprayed my pan with vegetable spray to keep it from sticking. The first plate was handed to

Robin and I went back for more. "…Linda what do you have on this..?"

"… Well only the usual eggs, cinnamon, vanilla and milk to dip the bread in, and then the syrup on top… "

"…well I am sorry, but this does not taste good at all…" so he spit it out. Robin never refuses food, so we pondered this for a while and discovered, I had not used vegetable spray but had used bug repellant on the pan. Both items were sitting on the counter side by side and were the same color. I, of course, have never lived that down in all our years of marriage.

Along the way we had bought Jeremy a four-wheeler. Well, of course, Robin needed to have the ability to ride this, also. So with a few adaptions he enjoyed himself in the mountains behind his home place. One evening, I came home from work to find him with the trailer hooked up to the van and the four-wheeler loaded ready to go (thanks to friends). He was smiling and said to me "…Let's go…".

"What are you up to Robin? "

"..Just get in and see..." Well he had made arrangements to borrow an additional four-wheeler for me and we went to the top of the mountain on a trail. Just the two of us rode with our sandwiches and drinks and we had a wonderful time riding those trails. It was a great date night for the two of us.

Just a few years ago, I came home from work to realize our driveway was all "messed" up. Rocks and mud were everywhere. Drainage ditches were cut down into the dirt for water to drain off. I was trying to remember if Robin had told me who might be coming to do this work, when from the side of the house came a skid loader. I took a double take to realize it was Robin in the driver's seat with the biggest smile on his face that I had seen in a very long time. The need was there and he saw that it was his responsibility to take control to fix not only our driveway, but taking the skid loader also to the farm for him to work various jobs there. Was there nothing he wouldn't try to do or accomplish? Nope! Even years later when the time came for us to remove some landscaping ties in our front yard because of rotting, he was the first one to volunteer to do the work and he did an outstanding job, too!

Many were the trips for us as we would go where God was directing Robin to go; to visit a church, or to go to a conference to hear various speakers that he grew to love. He wanted to glean and learn from each of them all that he could. His goal to be what God wanted him to be; to serve the Lord right where he was in that wheelchair. He would ask many questions and wait patiently while they would answer him. We were truly blessed to have met so many outstanding servants of the Lord. It seemed God placed us in so many favored positions. Many were the servants of God who became friends and prayer warriors alongside Robin.

I realized there were divine appointments for Robin in his life. Because of his personality and his sincerity for learning all God's Word, I saw Robin take the Bible as a way of life. Truly, he learned to see the best of all situations and to forgive as Christ would forgive. Sometimes it was just so simple; I had a hard time accepting some of those decisions in our marriage. I had to see the complications and the practicality in every choice. But ultimately God did rule in our marriage and that's what gave us the strength to continue day by day. I learned that usually the outcome would be good. We saw so many blessings in the decision that we would make. Teaching us through each other is what God was doing.

Thank you Father for all you have shown us!

CHAPTER 10

SAYING "YES" TO
THEIR NEEDS....

As I mentioned earlier, we shared our life with so many young people over the years. Robin was able to relate too many who were challenged with today's issues. Whether it was just as a friend or a father image, Robin would often have a "sidekick" as I called them. Many were the days of wood cutting or odd chores he would have them help him with and often I benefited from them, too. I was grateful for their help; sometimes they would stay for dinner. He usually repaid them with a ticket to a race or he took them on one of those trips where one would learn a history lesson along the way.

It seemed like many of the boys would come back and just enjoy time with Robin, maybe going on a hunting trip to the mountains or, better yet, they could ride along in the van with him on a cold windy hunting day. Since Robin had a license for hunting from the van, it became pretty obvious that some enjoyed being with him to keep warm. Groundhogs seemed to be fair game for all of them at any time of the year.

As we traveled on the road, someone recognizing Robin in the van would give us a wave of the hand. A teacher, friend or a mentor, he always knew who it was and could tell me a story of how or what they had done together.

When it came to a need for a work day at the church, he had the ability to line up and organize an entire crew. Many were the sore muscle of those who could not refuse a phone call from Robin. Usually, Robin, too, was on his John Deere tractor doing whatever he could to mow, rake, or haul the brush or stones to get the job done. Hours and hours he would be on that John Deere tractor. The license plate on the front of his Ford van read "My other vehicle is a John Deere".

If someone just needed a speaker to share his testimony, Robin was willing. I don't know that I ever heard him turn anyone away when he had an opportunity to share what God had done in his life. Likewise, to be a leader when needed, when he was asked to fulfill the position, he would say yes. He prayed early in his life to be used by God and said that he would always do for others whatever was possible. Sometimes he stretched that "possible" but God never let him down. God's promises to provide for Robin were always fulfilled.

As a family, Robin challenged us all with keeping up with him. But it was to our advantage to help him fulfill his roles that God would lay on his heart. We gained the friendship of many, learned to care about others, in seeing their needs before our own. We also learned to be sure that we do all that we can possibly do to make life a little easier for someone else. When life throws us off the course that God has for us, we regroup and go back to the starting point to see what we can do differently. Robin knew that even in a mistake, forgiveness was and is always available when we look to our Heavenly Father. No circumstance is beyond God's forgiveness. No circumstance is beyond a cry out to our Father God for help. He created us for His pleasure and for His fellowship. We need to remember, that he wants to help us, and God only wants the best for us. And that is what Robin believed and portrayed to all of us.

CHAPTER 11

OUR SPIRITUAL MENTOR

As our journey continued on this path that God walked us through, Robin and I focused on what God would have us bring to people who crossed our paths. To many, Robin would give his wisdom on how much God was doing for him in spite of being in a wheelchair. As Robin would say, "…God told me to get my eyes off myself and see what I could do for others…" And that is the life Robin led. Over the years Robin's faith grew and he knew to whom he belonged in Christ and from where his strength came. He was always encouraged by many spiritual leaders he would hear. I found much of Robin's life was led by what Jesus would say or do.

He and I often had our disappointments as our faith lived for a miracle to see Robin walk one day in this earthly realm. Our children grew up to believe that would take place one day. Often Robin's questions to various speakers, pastors and friends would be "…What do you see me doing wrong or what should I be doing differently…" He sincerely wanted to know how he should change his walk with the Lord or whether his life should be different in anyway. Never did he want to hinder others from their walk with the Lord. Never did he want placed on a pedestal above anyone, daily walking out a goal to be what God had called him to be. Was he perfect? No way! More than once he and I would have our disagreements or become disappointed in each other. But our love was strong and it kept us together.

I witnessed him calling people, even if it was the middle of the night, to ask for forgiveness if he felt something was said that may have resulted in hurt. He would get out of his wheelchair lay prostrate on our living room floor crying out to God for his directions and guidance. Occasionally, he would wheel down the road or go off in the van somewhere to seek God's perfect will in every decision that he would make. Never did he want to lose the favor of God on his life, finding comfort in praise and worship music and listening often to scriptures on tapes. Robin had an ability to retain those scriptures. He amazed me and many others. Often he would point out scriptures to help all of us when in the midst of a storm in our lives.

Robin was dedicated to his family and wanted more than anything to be not only a good dad but a spiritual mentor to them. As our family matured and got through those awkward, teenage years, Robin's spiritual guidance became an important part of our lives. By way of a phone call, or just example he became our spiritual mentor.

When Robin and I got married, it was for a lifetime of commitment. That was the vow we took before God, family and friends on May 10, 1980. To love and to honor in sickness and in health. Our life was not the dream that we had for ourselves. But in many ways God blessed us more than our dreams could take us with a home of love, laughter and faith. Yes, there were often tears and disappointment. But if we took our eyes off ourselves and placed them on someone else's problems, it would give us renewed goals and strength in the walk that God had given us. As our family has grown with both of our children now married and even with blessings of grandchildren, Robin's guidance continues.

Being so very proud of his children and all that they have accomplished, he was overjoyed. Seeing his grandchildren, often he would send up to heaven the prayers for them to be blessed. He made sure there were toy John Deere tractors and lots of hugs and kisses.

My journey of 33 years with this amazing man of God whom I was blessed to have called my husband will never be replaced. Nothing can ever take the place of fulfillment: full of purpose, love, spiritual growth and yes, an adventure of a lifetime. More than our dreams could ever have imagined, it was a journey designed by our Father in Heaven. We both had our faults in the way all humans have, never being perfect.

And our marriage was often challenged, but we are forgiven by the shed blood of Jesus Christ who died on the cross for all, Robin and me. We too often used the words, "I'm sorry. Please forgive me". And that is what allowed us to make it through a life of a different challenge.

As I finalize this amazing journey, I feel it was way too short. I want more, but God has found it time to end this life chapter. Remember earlier I defined the word "Home". Truly that is where Robin is now. Waiting and preparing for all of us on the day that we too will join him.

Robin's condition the last few weeks was unexpected and a puzzle in many ways. During this time we were in the hospital. He experienced for the first time in all these years, physical pain that was very exhausting and difficult on him. He became weaker as the days went by. It became hard for him to even talk with us without becoming short of breath. Still he tried his best to be upbeat to all those who came for a visit. One night I spent the night and as I sat by his bedside, he and I looked at each other. Still not realizing that we would be walking through our final days together, he said to me how nice it was for just us to be here together. And we really didn't need to talk. Just holding hands seemed to be enough. Just a couple days later we experienced Valentine's Day while there in the hospital. I gave him a huge balloon heart that said "I Love You" with a card, and he gave me a stuffed bear, perfume and a card. Sitting side by side there in his room we talked and shed some tears. We, as the family, saw the changes physically from then on. In only a few more days, as though he knew, my dear husband gave me another card and flowers for what would be the last that I would receive from him. It would be a private message of his devotion and love for me, for our lifetime together of memories.

Emergency surgery became necessary. The children and I were there when he came out and each had our moments with him. It would be the last night before he passed away. Elisha and I stayed by his side that night; it was still a blur. Jeremy arrived back in the morning. Not even then was I truly realizing we were ending our life journey together. On a ventilator, he knew Jeremy, Elisha and I were there but could not talk. By holding our hands on top of his as he moved his wrists, we knew he felt our presence. I do believe in those final hours that went by, it gave us and the rest of the family time with him and he knew we were all there. Elisha and her fiancée, Ryan were to be married at the end of the summer. Our pastor held a mock wedding ceremony by Robin's bed-side. And then all too soon he breathed his last breath on this earth and joined the angels into his next journey…"Home".

We now know that he is pain free and embarking on a new journey of understanding the fulfillment of walking in Heaven with the Father, seeing firsthand the goal that we all are set out to see as Christians: to find ourselves in the arms of the one who formed us and breathed into us the breath of life.

No other goal in this life can matter more than to know whom your Savior is and our purpose in this life as a testimony to those around us. To serve and to be a servant, I pray I can shine with the love of Jesus as Robin shined. I hope to do half of what he has fulfilled in the rest of my journey in this life, to forgive when it's not easy to forgive, to love when it's hard and people are unlovable, to see in each one of God's creation the very best, as Robin saw through the eyes of the Heavenly Father in each of us.

To God be the glory for the things He has done....!

I find my joy in knowing that one day soon, I will see your face again, and for you to be my escort... "home"... as we circle around the throne of our Lord and Savior and to see the Face of God together and say "...Holy, Holy, Holy is the Lamb of God...who was and is and always will be..."

I love you always and forever my dear sweet Robin!
Your Loving and devoted (rib) wife!
Linda
AMEN!

Jeremiah 28:11; ...For I know the plans I have for you, declares the Lord, plans for good and not for evil, to give you a future and a hope.

(1) Webster dictionary

LINDA'S HEART

I want to bring only honor to my Father in Heaven and to the way he has blessed me over the years, with thirty-three years of marriage to this amazing man of God, my husband. I want also to share in these pages the struggles physically, emotionally and spiritually that I myself experienced. I pray that this will be encouraging to others that may be facing similar circumstances.

I adored and loved my husband. During the weeks after the accident, just as one would think, my tears seemed to be constant. I struggled spiritually with all the thoughts of why God would have our family go through this, but then I would think of how God might use this bad situation and us to bring honor to Him.

Robin and I knew our walk with the Lord was what would get us through each day. As he and I would pray together, and cry together, it gave me the extra push I needed to face each new day. I knew as long as we could communicate between each other and share our thoughts I could make it.

I was a strong person and one could say "stubborn", but that came from my struggles even before Robin and I were married. During my young adult life, I was pretty much left to make my own path. Little did I know that this was to help me to be a stronger woman now in the face of a challenging marriage.

When I met and married Robin, I looked forward to the papered side of being a woman: the romance and the perfect dream of a happy life ever after. I did have all of that from Robin on the romance side. The early years when our children were born, those moments were precious. As we built our home together, it was special. When we would go out together, Robin would open the door for me. He would take my hand and walk side by side with me: but our perfect dream changed and I, too, had to go back to the strong woman. We readjusted and were forced to do things differently. We would still hold hands as often as we could, steal a kiss even if it was in public. I wanted the world to know just how much I loved this man even though our lives had been turned upside down.

Yes, the responsibilities seem to be resting on my shoulders now, but Robin knew and understood. I wanted to keep him going and to be active, but both of us wanted to be a light so that God would shine through us.

I treasured the gift that God gave me in Robin. I did not take it lightly, our love for one another. He shared his dreams and desires with me, and I shared mine with him: that's what made our marriage strong.

Nahum 1:7 (NIV)
The Lord is good, a refuge in times of trouble,
He cares for those who trust in Him.

There is no one like the Lord! He will never leave us. He is always there to pick us up. When our human side weakens; and we lose control, that becomes the best time for the Lord to show himself to us. God does want only the best for us. But, unfortunately we live in a world of sin and hardships.

Sometimes I would feel so alone. For days I allowed the responsibilities to become more important than my time spent with the Lord. And this would only bring tears and questions, allowing for a wall to be built around myself that I thought I was using as protection. All I accomplished was to block out Robin and that brought hurt to me.

Ps. 46:10 (NIV)
Be still and know that I am God; I will be exalted among
the nations, I will be exalted in the earth.

As I realized that God would be exalted in all that we were facing, I would cry out to Him for forgiveness and then also to Robin, breaking down the wall. My most precious moments were the times when Robin would hold me at night as we prayed together. We exalted God in our lowest moments; my strength would then be renewed.

I had trust in the Lord that what I felt and went through would make me stronger and that He would not give me more than I could handle.

God is always there, He wants that trust from us. Just as an earthly father wants the trust of his children, so does our Heavenly Father. As children run to the safe haven of their father's open arms, so God our Heavenly Father wants the same for us.

Many times my stubbornness held me back from running to those open arms of my Heavenly Father. I felt I needed to do it on my own. But I would finally cry out to the Father and he would see me through.

The journey was hard at times. But with the "three" of us; Father God, Robin and I, we ran the race. We set out for the goal. Father God helped Robin to the finish line and he has won. Now alone with my journey I will continue the race to the goal. And with the help of my Father we will make it together. As the years have taught me He will not leave me or forsake me as I walk daily towards finishing the race.

What is the goal; to spend eternity with Father God in Heaven and until I arrive there, I will be a Christ-like example to all those around me. Living a full life here where I am at. With Father God as my guide I will strive to be all that He desires of me.

Prayer……Father in Heaven, I pray for this opportunity you have given to me; that I will glorify you in all I say and do. That I walk in your love to be a light for those around me. And for each one that has read this book to see how short life can be and how quickly changes come; knowing that you are here for all and that you have every circumstance, and challenge in control. Let them feel your presence at this very moment. I ask you to send someone across their path to walk with them Father. Give to them a spiritual mentor. I pray this prayer and trust you to fulfill in them your goals for this life, but to run the race to the finish line…

In your precious name of Jesus I pray! Amen.

2Timothy 4:7&8 (NIV)
I have fought the good fight, I have finished the race, and I have kept the faith. Now there is in store for me the crown of righteousness which the Lord, the righteous Judge will award to me on that day and not only to me, but also to all who have longed for his appearing.

Here are some Scriptures I hope will help and encourage you. (NIV)

When Strength is needed:
Ps. 28:7 ...The Lord is my strength and my shield; my heart trusts in him...
Ps. 118:14 ...The Lord is my strength and my defense; he has become my salvation.
Isaiah 12: 2 ... Surely God is my Salvation; I will trust and not be afraid, The Lord, The Lord himself, is my strength
Philippians. 4:13 ...I can do all things through Christ who Strengthens me.

When Joy is needed:
Nehemiah 8:10 Do not grieve; the Joy of the Lord is your strength.
Ps 19:8 The precepts of the Lord are right, giving joy to the heart.
Ps 95:1 Come let us sing for the Joy to the Lord.

When you have Fear:
Ps. 27:1... The Lord is my light and my salvation – whom shall I fear- the Lord is the stronghold of my life.
Ps. 27:3 ... Though an army besiege me, my heart will not fear: though war break out against me, even then I will be confident.

Ps. 34:4 ... I sought the Lord, and he answered me; he delivered me from all my fears.

I John 4:18...There is no fear in love. But, perfect love drives out fear because fear has to do with punishment. The one who fears is not made perfect in love.

When you need Love:

Deuteronomy 11:13... To Love the Lord your God, and to serve Him with all your heart and with all your soul.

I Corinthians 13:4 Love is patient, love is kind

I Corinthians 13:13 and now these three remain; faith, hope and love, but the greatest of these is love.

Galatians 5:22 But the fruit of the Spirit is love, joy, peace, forbearance, kindness, goodness, faithfulness

Ephesians 5:2 ...and walk in the way of love, just as Christ loved us and gave himself up for us.

And last of all as man and wife:

Ephesians 5:25 ...husbands love your wife as Christ loves the church....

Ephesians 5:33 ...love his wife as he loves himself, and the wife must respect her husband.

To sum up a successful relationship.

As much as Robin and I loved each other, we did also respect one another. Love, Respect, Honor and Cherish.

Communicate and pray together. Never loose site or direction of the goal set before you. To Honor each other and God every day in all you say and do.

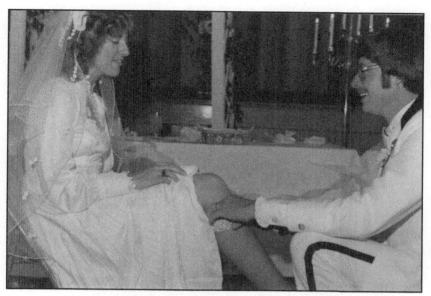

WEDDING DAY MAY 10 1980

WEDDING DAY

JEREMY HELPING HIS DAD DRIVE IN UTAH

ELISHA HELPING HER DAD DRIVE IN UTAH

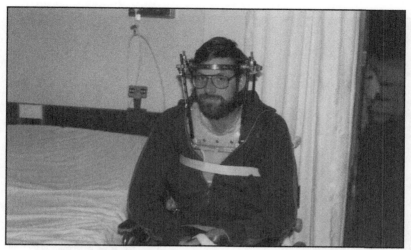

ROBIN AFTER GETTING HIS HALO VEST

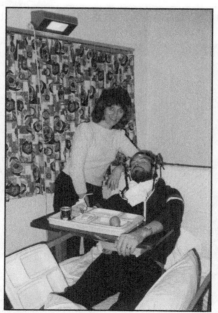

ROBIN AND LINDA WHILE IN THE
REHABILITATION CENTER

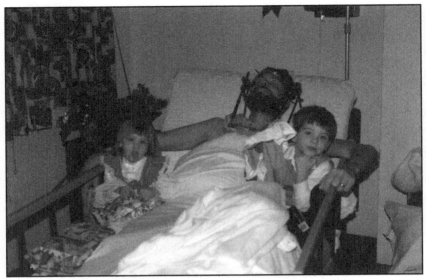

ELISHA ROBIN AND JEREMY CHRISTMAS 1985
WHILE IN REHABILITATION

ROBIN DURING HUNTING SEASON. FIRST DOE 1988

ROBIN S 8PT AND JEREMY S 4 POINT. TOGETHER IN 2003

ROBIN COACHING JR HIGH BOYS BASKETBALL

ROBIN INSTRUCTING THE TEAM

FEIGHT FAMILY

CAMPING WITH BUDDIES AND A GOOD LAUGH

ROBIN PLOWING SNOW ON HIS JOHN DEERE TRACTOR

ROBIN AND LINDA HIKING

ROBIN COCO CAY

Robin Reed Feight

Robin driving the skid loader

Carolina Beach vacation

NHRA Races

Family on the Wedding day for our
daughter September 7 2013

CPSIA information can be obtained at www.ICGtesting.com
Printed in the USA
BVOW09s2349300914

368942BV00027B/451/P